KU-033-233

Collins

PRIMARY WRITING

BOOK 2

John Jackman
Wendy Wren

Collins Educational
An imprint of HarperCollinsPublishers

Published by Collins Educational
An imprint of HarperCollins*Publishers* Ltd
77-85 Fulham Palace Road
London W6 8JB

© John Jackman and Wendy Wren 1998

First published 1998
Reprinted 1999
ISBN 0 00 302339 7

John Jackman and Wendy Wren assert the moral right to be identified as the authors of this work.

Illustrations by Kathy Baxendale, Maggie Brand, Rob Englebright, Bethan Matthews, Andrew Midgley, Rhiannon Powell, Lisa Smith.

All rights reserved. No part of this publication may be reproduced, stored in a retrieval system, or transmitted in any form or by any other means, electronic, mechanical, photocopying, recording or otherwise, without either the prior permission of the Publisher or a licence permitting restricted copying in the United Kingdom issued by the Copyright Licensing Agency Ltd, 90 Tottenham Court Road, London W1P 9HE.

British Library Cataloguing in Publication Data
A catalogue record for this book is available from the British Library.

Cover illustration: Andrew Midgley
Editor: Mitzi Bales
Designer: Neil Adams

Printed by Scotprint, Musselburgh

Acknowledgements
The author and publishers wish to thank the following for permission to use copyright material:
Egmont Children's Books Ltd for 'Sunning' from *Crickety Cricket* by James S Tippett, William Heinemann; Faber and Faber Ltd for 'Wolf' and 'December' from *Midnight Forest* by Judith Nicholls; Gervase Phinn for 'Seasonal Haiku' by Richard Matthews, 'Yeti' by Gervase Phinn, 'Mark' by Helen White, and 'Dad' by Collette Chapple from *Lizard Over Ice* by Gervase Phinn, Nelson, 1990; Vernon Scannell for 'My Dog', 1996; Royal Geographic Society, London, for photograph of Norgay and Hillary; Papilio for photograph of Mount Everest.

Every effort has been made to trace the copyright holders, but if any have been inadvertently overlooked, the publishers will be pleased to make the necessary arrangement at the first opportunity.

Contents

Thinking about characters

This story helps you think about the way a writer can make you like or dislike a character.

Sir Clifford Marsden is a young boy when Henry VIII is on the throne. He first meets the king when Henry VIII comes to Marsden Hall.

My tutor had told me legends from Ancient Greece and I'd heard about the gods on Mount Olympus. When I first set eyes on King Henry VIII, I'll swear I believed he was one of those gods come down to earth. Perhaps my childish mind was right – for the gods were wonderfully beautiful, but utterly cruel and selfish. And so was Henry.

That afternoon he was wearing plain green hunting clothes. I was disappointed to see that he was not wearing his crown. But as he jumped down from his horse I saw that he was a giant of a young man. And it wasn't just looking up at him as a child that made him seem so huge. It was a simple fact: Henry was the tallest man I have ever met – six foot three inches or more.

The king had red-gold hair and rose coloured skin as fine as any woman's. His bright blue eyes were fierce and restless. I know now that they were just a little too close together and that his soft mouth was just a little too small under the neat red beard. But when I first saw him I thought he was the handsomest man in the world.

Many years later, Sir Clifford is summoned to see the king. By this time King Henry had divorced his first wife, Catherine of Aragon, and is married to Anne Boleyn.

King Henry was as changed as Catherine of Aragon. His fine body had become bloated

Making the reader dislike Henry

Many details about his looks

Adjectives give a clear picture

A strong word; not just 'fat'

and his handsome face almost square. Those eyes that had been thought too small before were sunk in folds of fat now and edged with red. His whole face was too red, in fact, and the golden beard was darker. The blond hair was thin, and his baldness covered with a hat that dripped pearls. "You've a letter, Marsden," he said. His breath was short.

> Alliteration catches attention

> Unusual description

from *The King in Blood Red and Gold* by Terry Deary

Think about it

1. Read the descriptions carefully of Henry VIII as a young man and as an older man.
   Copy and complete the chart.

Words and phrases which describe the young Henry	Words and phrases which describe the older Henry

2. Write a short paragraph to say if you like or dislike Henry. Give your reasons.

Now try these

1. Imagine you are going to write a story in which there are two brothers **or** two sisters.
   You want your readers to like one of your characters and dislike the other.
   Write a description of each of your characters so that your readers respond as you want them to.
   Remember to include what the characters look like and what sort of person they are.

2. Choose a character that you disliked **or** felt sorry for from a book that you have read.
   Write a description of the character and say how the writer made you dislike them **or** feel sorry for them.

This story presents a problem for the main character. What would you have done in his place?

The story takes place in the early nineteenth century. Farm workers were then very poorly paid. Some of the men in Winterstoke village have been holding secret meetings to form a Trade Union and protest against such low pay. One of these men is Thomas Leggat but Daniel, a kitchen boy, discovers he is a spy.

> A question starts the reader wondering

There on the path stood Squire Plumtree himself, in his high polished boots and starched white neckcloth, talking to a man who wore the rough clothes of a labourer. Daniel recognised him at once – it was Thomas Leggat, one of the men whom Daniel had seen at the secret ceremony. Why would the Squire stand talking secretly in the cold darkness to a mere farm worker unless...? Daniel started to shiver.

The man glanced round nervously as he spoke, his eyes glinting in the light from the window like those of an animal at bay.

> Is Daniel cold or frightened?

The Squire had a peculiar look of pleasure on his face – not the kind that comes from happiness, but the kind which stems from black, grim satisfaction, as when an opponent has been defeated. Daniel strained his ears to hear.

'...and so it is all arranged, and I suggest to you that you keep yourself indoors,' the Squire was saying.

'Aye, master,' mumbled Leggat.

'That will be all then... Oh, and here's payment for you.'

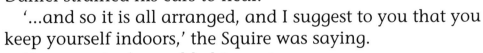

> Will Daniel be discovered?

At that moment – he could not help it – Daniel sneezed. Both men whirled round.

'Who's hiding there, in the name of God?' called the Squire in a furious voice.

Daniel stepped forward into the light. 'It's only me, your worship, with a letter from my master.'

Daniel knows there is another secret meeting tonight and he wants to warn the others that Squire Plumtree knows about it. When the Squire says he can go, he leaves with all speed.

Just as he reached the gates, however, a figure stepped out from the deeper blackness which encircled them, a figure which had been hiding in the thick bushes by the Manor entrance. It was a man – a tall man who reached out a strong, bony hand which gripped Daniel painfully by the neck. He wriggled but the grip tightened – viciously. And then a rough voice growled, 'Now my young master, my little listener, I be wanting you to tell me where you're rushing off to, like.' The tone was low and menacing, and as Daniel recognised it, his knees seemed to turn to water. It was Thomas Leggat – the man he now knew to be a spy.

Shows why Daniel might be afraid

Describes Daniel's feeling

from The Stove Haunting by Bel Mooney

Think about it

1. Write a word or phrase to describe how you think Daniel is feeling when:
    a) he 'strained his ears to hear'
    b) he sneezed
    c) Squire Plumtree let him go
    d) Thomas Leggat grabbed him by the neck.
2. Write about what you would have done in Daniel's place:
    a) when the Squire discovered him
    b) when Thomas Leggat caught him.

Now try these

1. Imagine you are Daniel. You know that if your friends are discovered, they will be put in prison.
    Write about how you got away from Leggat and what you did next.
2. Write about a time when you have been very frightened. How did you feel and what did you do?

UNIT 3

Writing a playscript

Here is a playscript made from a famous story. It shows you how a scene is built up.

Alice has fallen down a rabbit hole into a very strange sort of place. She has met some very odd characters and, at this point in the play, seems to be lost.

Scene 5: In a wood

> The scene setting; the stage will look like this

> Spoken words are called dialogue

Cheshire Cat: Miaw!

(Alice looks up. The Cheshire Cat is on a branch above her.)

Alice: Cheshire Puss!

(The Cheshire Cat grins. She crosses to the left of the Cheshire Cat.)

> Stage directions tell where characters are and what they do

> No speech marks in a playscript

Would you tell me please which way I ought to go from here?

> Names of characters with each speech

Cheshire Cat: That depends on where you want to go.

Alice: I don't care where...

Cheshire Cat: Then it doesn't matter which way you go.

Alice: What sort of people live about here?

Cheshire Cat: In one direction lives a Hatter, and in the other direction a March Hare. Visit either you like: they're both mad.

Alice: But I don't want to go among mad people.

Cheshire Cat: Oh, we're all mad here. You're mad. I'm mad.

Alice: How do you know that you're mad?

Cheshire Cat: To begin with, a dog's not mad. You grant that?

Alice: I suppose so.

Cheshire Cat: Well then, you see, a dog growls when it's angry, and wags its tail when it's pleased. Now I growl when I'm pleased and wag my tail when I'm angry.

Alice: I call it purring, not growling.

Cheshire Cat: Call it what you like! Do you play croquet with the Queen today?

Alice: I haven't been invited yet.

Cheshire Cat: You'll see me there.

(*The Cat vanishes.*)

adapted from *Alice's Adventures in Wonderland*, dramatised by Clemence Dane

Think about it

1. Write a description of the wood where Alice meets the Cheshire Cat so that the stage will look exactly as you want it to.

2. Add stage directions telling the actors how to say these lines:

Alice: (_____)

   Would you tell me please which way I ought to go from here?

Cheshire Cat: (_____)

   That depends on where you want to go.

Alice: (_____)

   But I don't want to go among mad people.

Cheshire Cat: (_____)

   Oh, we're all mad here. You're mad, I'm mad.

Now try these

1. Look at these sentences. Write them out as a playscript.

   Horace was very cross. "Bother, bother!" he said as he waddled around the garden.
   "What's the matter?" asked Freddy, the huge blackbird that lived in the tall oak tree.
   "You are looking at a very unhappy hedgehog," sighed Horace. "I've forgotten how to roll into a ball. Look!"
   Horace tried to roll into a tight ball but he just kept falling over.

2. Find a book that you have enjoyed reading.
   Choose a part where some characters have a conversation.
   Write the conversation as a playscript.

These poems show you how two different poets write about the same topic in their own way.

We see the dog through the owner's eyes

A more interesting word than "sits"

Similes help to give descriptions

My dog

My dog belongs to no known breed,
A bit of this and that.
His head looks like a small haystack.
He's lazy, smelly, fat.

If I say, 'Sit' he walks away.
When I throw a stick or ball
He flops down on the grass as if
He had no legs at all.

Lines two and four rhyme

And looks at me with eyes that say,
'You threw the thing, not me.
You want it back, then get it back.
Fair's fair you must agree.'

He is a thief. Last week but one
He stole the Sunday Roast.
And showed no guilt at all as we
Sat down to beans on toast.

The only time I saw him run –
And he went like a flash –
Was when a mugger in the park
Tried to steal my cash.

My loyal brave companion flew
Like a missile to the gate
And didn't stop till safely home.
He left me to my fate.

And would I swap him for a dog
Obedient, clean and good,
An honest, faithful, lively chap?
Oh boy, I would! I would!

Vernon Scannel

Sunning

Poet may not be dog's owner

"ing" words make good adjectives

First two lines and last two lines rhyme

In middle, lines four and six rhyme

Old dog lay in the summer sun
Much too lazy to rise and run.
He flapped an ear
At a buzzing fly,
He winked a half-opened
Sleepy eye.
He scratched himself
On an itching spot,
As he dozed on the porch
Where the sun was hot.
He whimpered a bit
From force of habit
While he lazily dreamed
Of chasing a rabbit.
But old dog happily lay in the sun
Much too lazy to rise and run.

James S. Tippett

Think about it

1. Read the poem 'My Dog'.
   Write the pairs of rhyming words.
   The first pair has been done to help you: that/fat
2. Read the poem 'Sunning'. Write the pairs of rhyming words.
3. In your own words explain how the dogs in the two poems are different.
4. Which poem do you like best? Give your reasons.

Now try these

Many poems use powerful words in their descriptions.
Make word webs by adding interesting words around each animal's name to show how the animal sounds and moves.

lion   cobra

Use your word web to write a poem about one of the animals.

Writing a newspaper report

Here are the notes a reporter made about a hospital fete. Notes like these help you plan your writing.

> Headings help to plan notes

> Notes about the setting

> Notes about what happened

Event:
Caversham Hospital annual summer fete

Weather:
started hot and sunny, not a cloud in the sky until wind and thunder storm came up suddenly.

Attendence:
very well attended, hospital grounds full of adults (including nurses and doctors), children and lots of grandparents too!

Purpose:
to collect money for equipment for the children's ward; raised over £3500

Activities:
Army parachute display team – difficult jump because of windy conditions, though all but one parachutist landed on the target. The one who missed finished in the hospital car park with parachute caught on a lamppost.
Mini motor bike racing – nasty crash but doctors and nurses quickly on scene and no serious injuries, though one child taken into the hospital!
Many other stalls and sideshows, including bouncy castle, always a favourite, welly throwing, tombola, wet-sponge throwing at the hospital administrator (seemed lots of the nurses were getting their own back)

Think about it

You are the reporter who made these notes.
Now write your report for your newspaper.

1. Set the scene. Write an opening paragraph
   to tell your readers the most important details.
   Say what the event was, and where, when
   and why it took place.
2. Write two or three other interesting paragraphs.
   Each paragraph should tell about something
   different and interesting.
3. Think of a catchy headline.

Now try these

1. The editor of your paper was pleased with your report,
   but only has space for an article of 50 to 60 words.
   Rewrite your report to fit the space.
2. The editor liked your headline, but would like to see some more
   ideas. Write three or four more possible headlines for your report.
3. The army would like you to write a separate report for their
   magazine. Write about the fete, but in a way that says much more
   about what the army magazine readers might be interested in.

Writing instructions

These instructions are clear and easy to follow, as such directions must be.

Making a hovercraft

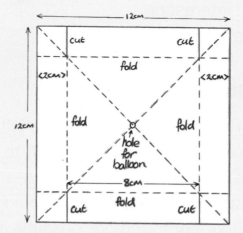

Diagram gives clear plan

Equipment list

You will need:
- stiff paper
- scissors
- sticky tape
- a balloon
- paints or colouring pens

Step by step instructions

What to do:
1. Cut a piece of paper 12 cm × 12 cm.
2. Measure 2 cm from each of the four sides and draw lines.
3. Find the centre of the paper by drawing two diagonal lines. Where they meet is the centre.
4. In the centre cut a hole about the size of a 20p coin.
5. Make four short cuts, one on each corner, as shown on the diagram.
6. Colour your hovercraft.
7. Fold in the corners as shown to make a box shape.
8. Use the sticky tape to hold the corners in position.
9. Pull the balloon through the hole and blow it up from underneath.

Think about it

Write instructions for making a model of something else. You can choose something yourself, or try to work out how this candle clock might be made.

Your instructions should have:
- a description of what the object is
- everything needed to make it
- clear, step-by-step instructions
- a diagram or picture, if this will help.

Now try these

Instructions are often needed for other reasons, apart from making things. Try to write instructions for one or both of these reasons.

a) Write instructions for a friend who is coming to your house for the first time. Write the instructions as if you are speaking to your friend.
   You may need to draw a map.

b) Write instructions for how to bath a dog.

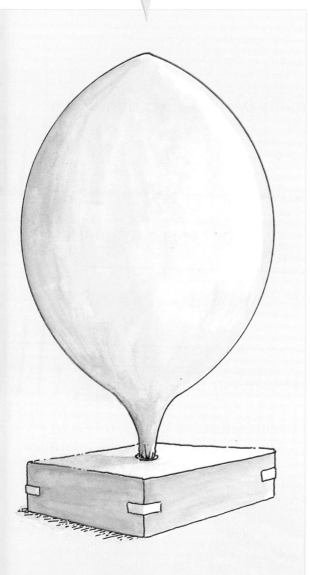

Picture of completed model

Other ideas:
Try making some hovercraft of other shapes and sizes.

Organising reports

This shows you how headings and lists can help make a report easy to read and understand.

Collecting leaves

Collecting can be fun, and many people collect things as a hobby. Some people collect:

- stamps
- coins
- stickers
- models
- dolls
- bracelet charms.

> Lists make it easy to read and check

Some people collect leaves because they are pretty and easy to find. Leaves can be found in:

- gardens
- parks
- streets with trees and bushes
- the school grounds.

> Headings help find information

How to start a collection

Collect leaves from trees and bushes and put them in a small box to save them.

Then place your leaves between sheets of paper, a few at a time. Press them under a heavy object for several days.

> Picture gives more details

Mounting your collection

Make a book for your collection or use a scrapbook.

When the leaves have been thoroughly pressed, mount them in your book with little pieces of sticky tape.

Decide how to organise your book.
You can sort your leaves by:

1. size
2. shapes
3. textures (smooth, hairy, prickly, rough)
4. colour

Research

To learn more about leaves, use reference books to find the names of your leaves. Label them neatly.

Think about it

Write a description of your own hobby or one you are interested in.
Set it out like the description for making a leaf collection.
Use:

• headings
• lists with dots like this list
• a diagram or picture, if this will help.

Now try these

Imagine that you have been put in charge of organising a survey of the plants, trees and creatures in the school grounds.
Use these ideas to help you make headings, notes and lists about the task. You may have other ideas as well.

Date and season   Equipment that will be needed
Jobs that will need to be done   People you will ask to help

Story settings

In this story you will see how you can build up the setting of a story with careful details.

Setting is not in real world

Typical characters in imaginary adventure

Bilbo Baggins is a hobbit who lives in the imaginary land of Middle Earth. He finds himself taken away from his comfortable home by Gandalf the wizard and a band of dwarves who are seeking the treasure guarded by Smaug the Magnificent, a very large and dangerous dragon.

Friendly setting differs from what is to come

At first they passed through hobbit-lands, a wide respectable country inhabited by decent folk, with good roads, an inn or two, and now and then a dwarf or a farmer ambling by on business. Then they came to lands where people spoke strangely, and sang songs Bilbo had never heard before. Now they had gone on far into the Lone-lands where there were no people left, no inns,

Name gives an idea of the setting

and the roads grew steadily worse. Not far ahead were dreary hills, rising higher and higher, dark with trees. On some of them were old castles with an evil look, as if they had been built by wicked people. Everything seemed gloomy, for the weather that day had taken a

Bad weather adds to frightening setting

nasty turn. Mostly it had been as good as May can be, even in merry tales, but now it was cold and wet. In the Lone-lands they had been obliged to camp when they could, but at least it had been dry...

Still the dwarves jogged on, never turning round or taking any notice of the hobbit. Somewhere behind the grey clouds the sun must have gone down, for it began to get dark as they went down into a deep valley with a river at the bottom. Wind got up, and willows along its banks bent and sighed. Fortunately the road went over an ancient stone bridge, for the river, swollen with the rains, came rushing down from the hills and mountains in the north.

Adds to the mystery and danger

Trees seem alive

From *The Hobbit* by J. R. R. Tolkien

Think about it

1. Pick out the words and phrases which describe the hobbit-lands.
2. How would you feel if you were with Bilbo Baggins in the hobbit-lands?
3. Pick out the words and phrases which describe the Lone-lands.
4. How would you feel if you were with Bilbo Baggins in the Lone-lands?

Now try these

1. Choose one of the following:
    a beach   a forest   a mountain top
    Write two short descriptions.
    a) One when the weather is warm and pleasant.
    b) One when the weather is cold and stormy.
2. Imagine what the next stage of Bilbo's journey might be.
    Remember that this is set in the imaginary world of Middle Earth.
    Write a description of the next land Bilbo might journey through.

This old poem introduces you to words not often used today.

> Short for "it is" in old language

> Older word for "middle"

> Old way to say "it was"

Try again

King Bruce of Scotland flung himself down
    In a lonely mood to think;
'Tis true he was monarch, and wore a crown,
    But his heart was beginning to sink.

For he had been trying to do a great deed,
    To make his people glad;
He had tried and tried, but couldn't succeed
    And so he became quite sad.

• • •

Now just at that moment a spider dropped,
    With its silken, flimsy clue;
And the King, in the midst of his thinking, stopped
    To see what the spider would do.

'Twas a long way up to the ceiling dome,
    And it hung by a rope so fine;
That how it would get to its cobweb home,
    King Bruce could not divine.

It soon began to cling and crawl
    Straight up with strong endeavour:
But down it came with a slippery sprawl,
    As near to the ground as ever.

• • •

Its head grew steady – again it went,
    And travelled a half-yard higher;
'Twas a delicate thread it had to tread,
    And a road where its feet would tire.

Again it fell and swung below,
    But again it quickly mounted;
Till up and down, now fast, now slow,
    Nine brave attempts were counted.

> A narrative poem tells a story

> Old fashioned word

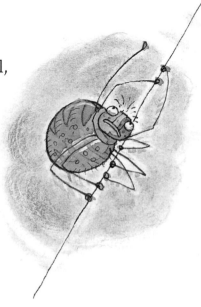

"Sure," cried the King, "that foolish thing
　　Will strive no more to climb;
When it toils so hard to reach and cling,
　　And tumbles every time."

. . .

Steadily, steadily, inch by inch,
　　Higher and higher he got;
And a little bold run at the very last pinch
　　Put him in his native cot.

"Bravo, bravo!" the King cried out,
　　"All honour to those who try;
The spider up there defied despair;
　　He conquered, and why shouldn't I?"

. . .

> Old fashioned phrase

Eliza Cook

Think about it

1.　Some of the words in the poem are not used very often today. Try to work out the meaning of the words in very black type by reading the whole verse and thinking about the sense. Then tick the meaning you think each word has.

a)　'King Bruce could not **divine**'
　　☐ guess　　☐ hope

b)　When it **toils** so hard to reach and cling'
　　☐ climbs　　☐ works hard

c)　Put him in his **native cot**'
　　☐ home　　☐ school

2.　In your own words, write the story that the poem tells.

Now try these

Choose any historical event you know about and write a poem of at least two verses.

Each verse must have four lines.

Lines 1 and 3 must rhyme and lines 2 and 4 must rhyme.

Try to use some of the old fashioned words and phrases from 'Try Again'.

More story settings

This picture can be used as a setting for your story.

Adjectives describe something	Adjective phrases are groups of words that describe something	Similes are phrases that use "as" and "like" to describe something

silent
still
motionless
dark
blue
brown
featureless
mysterious
desolate
strange

dark and frightening

vast, desolate expanse

fragile, blue earth

brown and dusty

as black as pitch
  (the sky)
as fragile as a bubble
  (the earth)
as fine as talcum powder
  (the dust)
as blue as the sea
  (the earth)
as silent as the grave
  (the atmosphere)

Think about it

1. Choose three adjectives from the list.
   Put each adjective into a sentence to describe the picture.
2. Choose three adjective phrases from the list.
   Put each adjective phrase into a sentence to describe the picture.
3. Choose three similes from the list.
   Put each simile into a sentence to describe the picture.
4. Write three adjectives, three adjective phrases and three similes
   of your own to describe the picture.

Now try these

1. Imagine you are inside the picture.
   You begin to walk across the moon's surface.
   Write about your thoughts and feelings.
2. You are going to write a story which is set on an imaginary planet.
   Write the beginning of the story by giving the reader a detailed
   description of what your planet looks like.

Writers have to correct their work to improve it. This shows you some of the things you can do.

The astronaut looked around him

Don't say the same thing twice

~~and looked~~ at the strange world. ~~It was~~

~~very strange.~~ There was no movement

and not a sound could be heard.

Use pronouns instead of repeating nouns

He
~~The astronaut~~ was standing on green

It
rock which glowed. ~~The green rock~~

stretched as far as he could see.

Add adverbs to show how things are being done

He took a few steps forward/ ~~He was~~

cautiously
~~cautious~~ because he did not know what

to expect. The ground seemed firm/ *but*

Use conjunctions to join sentences

with
~~When he took~~ his next step he sank into

It came
green sand. ~~He sank~~ over his boots

Use interesting verbs

he struggled
and ~~it was hard~~ to lift his feet up.

The astronaut looked around him at the strange world. There was no movement and not a sound could be heard.

He was standing on green rock which glowed. It stretched as far as he could see.

He took a few steps forward cautiously, because he did not know what to expect. The ground seemed firm, but with his next step he sank into green sand. It came over his boots and he struggled to lift his feet up.

Think about it

1. Rewrite these sentences to avoid repetition:
   a) The astronaut climbed out of the spacecraft and the astronaut looked around.
   b) The ground was brown and dusty and it was a brownish colour.
   c) He walked away from the spacecraft and walked over to a large rock.
2. Add words to these sentences so they do not begin with 'It was'. The first one has been done for you.
   a) It was silent on the moon.   *No sound was heard on the moon.*
   b) It was easy to move about.
   c) It was the first time he had been to the moon.
3. Add or change some words to make these sentences more interesting.
   a) The ground was flat.
   b) He wanted to walk across the moon.
   c) He jumped in the air.

Now try these

1. Write a first draft to continue the story so the reader knows what happens to the astronaut. Leave a space between each line of your story.
2. When you have finished, go back and edit your story to improve it. It is easier to do your editing in a different coloured pen.

Making notes

There are many ways of making notes to help you write reports and stories. The activities will ask you to try several ways, using this report.

<u>Mount Everest</u>, at 8840m (29,002 feet or about 5.5 miles), is the <u>highest mountain</u> in the world. It is part of a range of very high mountains to the north of India called the <u>Himalaya</u>. These mountains are in Nepal and Tibet. They are so high that they are <u>always covered in snow and ice</u>. There is very <u>little oxygen</u> at these high altitudes, so climbers need to carry supplies of oxygen in tanks on their backs. **1**

Key words and phrases underlined

The mountain was named after Sir George Everest, who was the first to measure its height in 1849. **2**

In the 1920s and 1930s many teams of climbers attempted to reach the peak. All of these teams were helped by Sherpa people, who live in the mountains and know them well. They acted as porters, carrying food, tents and tanks of oxygen. **3**

In 1952 a Sherpa called Tenzing Norgay worked with a Swiss expedition that climbed within 200m of the summit. This team had to turn back because of cold and **4**

A good picture says more than a hundred words

Each paragraph adds information

Maps are another way to give information

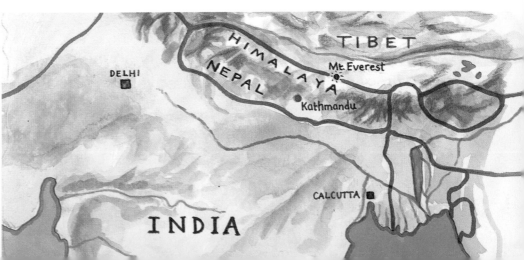

exhaustion, but Tenzing learned a great deal from this experience. In 1953 he helped the British team succeed in reaching the summit. The team was led by John Hunt, but Tenzing Norgay and Edmund Hillary were the first at the top on 29 May 1953.

Teams still try to reach the summit today. Sadly, many are killed in the attempt. Some do succeed, though. In 1975 a group of Japanese women made the ascent and one of them, Junko Tabei, was the first woman to reach the summit.

5

Think about it

1. Copy this chart. Fill in the events that happened in the years shown.

1849	
1920s & 1930s	
1952	
1953	
1975	

2. Next to each paragraph is a small number.
   Write a list of the key words and phrases in each paragraph.
   The first paragraph is done to help you.

   1 Mount Everest   highest mountain   Himalaya
   always covered in snow and ice   little oxygen

Now try these

1. Use your notes to write a shorter version, about half the size, of the information about Mount Everest. Try to keep all the most important information.
2. Find an information book on a subject that interests you. Read a section, make notes of the key words and phrases, and then write a summary.

A written explanation

Some reports explain an event or product, as this one shows.

Key words and phrases underlined

<u>Before printing</u> was invented, there were <u>only a few thousand books</u> in the whole world. Each book had to be <u>copied by hand</u>, so they took a long time and <u>cost a lot</u> of money. Most books were kept <u>in</u> the <u>libraries</u> of palaces, monasteries and universities. They would be <u>chained</u> to the <u>shelves</u> so that they couldn't be stolen.

Each paragraph gives new information

After printing was invented about 500 years ago, many more books were produced. Then many ordinary people wanted to learn to read.

About 250 years ago, storybooks began to be popular. Books were still too expensive for most people, but libraries were set up and people could borrow books. There was a charge for borrowing.

Books were also important in education. Text books were written for teaching in schools and colleges. This allowed many more people to be educated. As people became more educated, they became better able to invent and make things, to write books and to run better companies. This helped countries with good education systems to become world leaders.

One of the most important results of printing was the growth of daily newspapers. These let people know what was happening in the world away from their own village or town. It also let them begin to understand what the politicians were doing, and so ordinary people could give their opinion.

Some would say that printing has changed the world more than nearly any other invention.

Think about it

Explain why the invention of printing was so important.
Start each paragraph like this:

Paragraph 1 I think the invention of printing was important because _____

Paragraph 2 Before printing was invented _____

Paragraph 3 Printing changed people's lives in several ways.

      a) _____

      b) _____

      c) _____

Paragraph 4 That is why I think that the invention of printing was _____

Now try these

1. The writer has used nearly 250 words to say why the invention of printing was important. Write your own shorter version, using no more than 50 words. Try not to miss any of the most important points.

2. Some people might say that television is more important than printing. Which of the two do you think is more important? Give your reasons, setting your ideas out in paragraphs as you did in 'Think about it'.

Explaining how something works

This report explains the water cycle, using a diagram to help make it clear.

Information in paragraphs

Without water life would be impossible, so it is fortunate that water is one of the commonest substances on Earth.

The oceans cover about three-quarters of the Earth's surface. They are like huge reservoirs. Large amounts of water evaporates from the seas into the sky each day, and changes into clouds.

Information in diagram

The clouds move over the land areas and the water falls out, mainly in the form of rain or snow, which then runs into streams and rivers, then back into the oceans.

This process is called the water cycle.

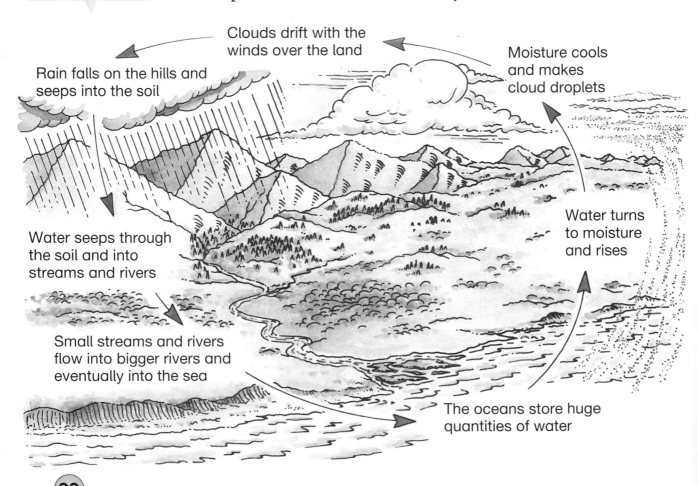

Clouds drift with the winds over the land

Moisture cools and makes cloud droplets

Rain falls on the hills and seeps into the soil

Water turns to moisture and rises

Water seeps through the soil and into streams and rivers

Small streams and rivers flow into bigger rivers and eventually into the sea

The oceans store huge quantities of water

Think about it

Look again at the diagram.
Write an explanation of the water cycle, without using a diagram.
Start like this:

Water is extremely important to us. Without it _____

These words and phrases might be helpful to make your account more interesting.

To begin with _____

After this _____

The next stage is _____

As a result of _____

Before the water can _____ it

Eventually it _____

Now try these

There are other cycles like the water cycle in nature. The growing cycle of a plant is another example. The plant makes a seed, the seed lands in the soil and grows, the new plant then makes its own seeds.

a) Draw a diagram to illustrate how a seed and plant goes through this cycle. Label each part of the diagram.

b) Write an explanation of the seed/plant cycle. Don't forget to mention important details such as when the plants need water or warm sunshine to help them grow.

UNIT 15 Problems in stories

This story shows how a writer presents the problem that the main character faces.

The beginning of Lucy's story is about her first days at a new school.

Tells feelings on starting a new school

It's crazy, starting a new school. For days you feel so new and lost it's as if you've wandered into a foreign country where you can't speak the language. Then, all of a sudden, everything falls into place and you feel you've been there for ever.

Gives different situations at school

The people fall into place too. It doesn't take long to work out who's going to be popular and who's going to be out of it, who's going to get into trouble and who's going to be teacher's pet.

It was obvious, from that very first day, that Rafaella was going to be an outsider, on the edge of everything, not liked. No one actually hurt or even teased her much. They just ignored her and left her out of things.

"What do you want, Earwig?" a group of girls would say, as Rafaella approached them.

They would stop their conversation to turn and look at her coldly, and she would blush, as she always did, mumble "Nothing," and turn away.

I was in those groups sometimes, trying to talk to Kate and Sophie, the two super-popular girls in the class. And I'd watch Rafaella and think, Not like that, you idiot. Smile. Say something cool. Don't show you care.

from *Secret Friends* by Elizabeth Laird

> This shows cruelty to Rafaella

> Rafaella is embarrassed

> Outwardly Lucy sides with the popular girls

> Inwardly Lucy would like to help Rafaella

Think about it

1. What do you think about the way the other girls treat Rafaella?
2. How do you think Rafaella should react when they are rude to her?
3. Lucy thinks Rafaella should, "Smile. Say something cool. Don't show you care."
   a) Do you agree? Give your reasons.
   b) How do you think Kate and Sophie would react if Rafaella behaved in this way?

Now try these

1. Imagine you are Rafaella.
   Write a letter to Lucy explaining how you feel when the girls are mean to you. Ask Lucy why she does not like you.
2. Imagine you are Lucy. One day, when Kate and Sophie are rude to Rafaella, you stick up for her.
   Write what you would say to show Kate and Sophie that the way they treat Rafaella is wrong.

A different ending

A story can end in many ways and a writer must decide which is best.

The story so far:

Paul, Mandy and Ali are the last to leave the classroom at playtime. When everyone comes back in, Kate's lunch-box is missing. The teacher questions the three children and, although Paul has taken the lunch-box, all three of them say they know nothing about it. They are sent to the Headteacher.

The writer wants you to dislike Paul and the Headteacher

Ending 1

"Well," said the Headteacher. "What can you tell me about Kate's lunch-box?"

"Nothing," said Mandy. "I don't know anything."

"And you, Paul? What do you know about it?"

"I saw Ali take it," said Paul.

"That's not true," shouted Ali. "I left the classroom before you did."

"Well, Ali," said the Headteacher, "If Paul says you took it then that must be right. I shall have to ring your mother."

The writer makes Paul and the Headteacher likeable

Ending 2

"Well," said the Headteacher. "What can you tell me about Kate's lunch-box?"

"Nothing," said Mandy. "I don't know anything."

"And you, Paul? What do you know about it?"

Paul just stood there, looking at the ground.

"I think Paul took it," said Mandy.

"So do I," said Ali. "He was the last in the classroom."

"Well, Paul? What do you say?"

"It was only a joke. I would have given it back."

"Well, Paul, you must return the lunch-box and you must apologise to Kate. We'll say no more about it this

time, but if you are ever involved in anything like this again I will have to tell your parents."

Ending 3

"Come in, all of you," said the Headteacher in a stern voice. "Now I understand that you have all been involved in taking someone's lunch-box."

"No, I wasn't involved," protested Mandy.

"Nor was I," said Ali. "The teacher asked us about it because we were the last in the classroom before playtime."

"I really don't care," said the Headteacher. "As far as I am concerned you are all to blame and you will all be punished!"

> The writer makes the Headteacher unpleasant

Think about it

1. Copy and complete the chart to show how the characters behave in each of the three endings to the story. Some examples have been done to help you.

	Paul	Mandy	Ali	Headteacher
Ending 1	He lies			
Ending 2		Says what she thinks		
Ending 3			Tries to explain	

2. Which ending do you think is the best one for the story? Why?

Now try these

1. Decide how you would like the reader to feel about each of the characters and write your own ending for the story.
2. Choose one of the following ideas and write your own ending:
   a) The Three Little Pigs: The wolf gets stuck in the chimney of the brick house.
   b) The Three Billy Goats Gruff: Big Billy Goat Gruff has started across the bridge. The troll is friendly.

Writing haiku

A haiku is a special kind of poem which comes from Japan.

A haiku always follows the same form

Mark

5 syllables in the first line

Hair a tangled mop
Broken teeth and runny nose
That's my brother Mark.

7 syllables in the second line

Helen White

5 syllables in the third line

Wolf

still on his lone rock
stares at the uncaged stars and
cries into the night

No rhyming

17 syllables altogether

Judith Nicholls

Seasonal Haiku

Pictures in words of each of the four seasons

Buds full, fat and green
Pink blossoms trembling on trees
The warm breath of SPRING.

A burnished brass face
In an empty, cloudless sky
Smiles with SUMMER heat.

This sets the scene

Curled and twisted leaves
Carpet red the cold dead earth.
AUTUMN'S withered hand.

This shows some action

This brings the two together

Bitter winds of ice
Brittle grass like icy spikes
Old soldier WINTER.

Richard Matthews

Think about it

1. Count the syllables in each line and write down the number.
   a) I wandered lonely as a cloud
   b) On either side the river lie
   c) The Roman Road runs straight and bare
2. Write a five syllable line about:
   a) a snowflake
   b) a train
   c) a hippopotamus
3. Which of the haiku in Unit 17 do you like best?
   Give your reasons.

Now try these

1. Write a haiku about a member of your family or a friend.
2. Choose the season you like best and write a haiku which will
   tell the reader why you like it.
3. Choose an animal you like and an animal that you don't like.
   Write a haiku about each animal without using the words 'I like'
   or 'I don't like'.
   See if a friend can say which animal you like and which animal
   you don't like by reading your haiku.

Acrostic poems

These poems show you how to spell a word with the first letter of each line.

Yeti

Can have only one word in each line

You
Enormous
Tibetan
Iceman

Gervase Finn

December

Water
Ices
Naked
Trees
Earth
Rests

Are often short word pictures

Judith Nicholls

Dad

Can have more than one verse

Dozing in his easy chair,
Asleep and snoring.
Deep in dreams of when he was young.

Dandruff on his collar
And an ever-growing paunch,
Drab old jumper and baggy pants.

Does he remember when I was little
And held his hand in the sand in the sun?
Does he know how I love him?

DAD of mine.

Collette Chapple

Think about it

1. Which acrostic do you like best?
   Give your reasons.

2. Copy out and finish these acrostics.
   a) **S**oft and white
      Nighttime covering
      On the ground
      W_____
   b) **S**lipping through my fingers
      And sticking to my toes
      N_____
      D_____

Now try these

1. Write an acrostic on the word RAINBOW.
   Use as many colour words as you can.

2. Write a two verse acrostic on one of these:
   a) a worm
   b) water
   c) the wind

3. Ask your friend for the name of
   an object with no more than
   five letters.
   Write an acrostic about it.

Points of view

Here is an editorial written for a local newspaper. An editorial writer can say what he or she thinks about something, rather than just reporting the facts of a story.

A statement of the point of view

Main reason

Other reasons

Conclusion

LOOKING AFTER OUR CHILDREN

This newspaper thinks that the Council should pay for more after-school clubs for our young people. We believe this would make life more interesting and enjoyable for our young people, and it would allow parents who are at work to know that their children are safe and being looked after.

Our main reason for suggesting more clubs is that there aren't many places where young people can play safely, especially games like football or rounders. In the winter, or when it's raining, many have nowhere to go except to the shopping centre. The clubs could offer indoor hobbies as well as outdoor games.

A further reason is that some children don't have a suitable place to get their homework done, for as soon as everyone gets home, on goes the television! The clubs could provide a quiet corner for doing homework.

Furthermore we believe that clubs would help parents who go to work and can't get home when school finishes. Many parents worry about their children's safety, but must work away from home to earn money for their families. After-school clubs would take away a lot of worry from a lot of people!

Therefore, although some people might argue that it would be expensive to run the after-school clubs, this newspaper believes that it would be money well spent.

Think about it

When we want to make someone agree with our point of view, it is important that we think carefully about what we write, and how we write it. Look at this question:

> Do you think fishing is cruel to fish and should be banned, or do you think fishing is a hobby that is fun for many people and should be allowed?

Write an editorial giving your point of view on fishing.
Start like this:

> Although not everyone would agree, I think that ....

You might find that these words and phrases at the beginning of each of your paragraphs will help you to organise your writing:

> I have several reasons for my point of view. My first reason is ...
>
> A further reason is ...
>
> Furthermore ...
>
> Therefore, although some people might say that ...
>
> I think I have shown that ...

Now try these

Pretend you are the editor of your local newspaper.
Write an editorial arguing for or against one of these:
a) Cars should be banned from all town centres.
b) Fox hunting is cruel and should be banned.
c) Children under 12 should not be out in the streets after dark.

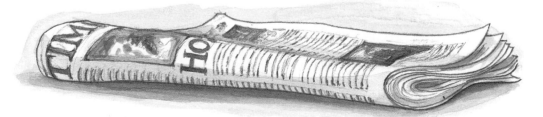

Letter of complaint

Have you ever felt cross about something, perhaps because something that you have bought doesn't work properly? Jennie's letter is an example of how you can write a letter to complain about it.

Address of writer

23 Centre Crescent
Upper Blaxland
Suffolk X1 2YY

Date

Wednesday 4th July

Person who is getting the letter

Dear Mr Smith,

States the general problem

Last week I bought a new bike from your shop. At first I was very pleased with it, but already things have started to go wrong. When I came into the shop to tell you about it, the assistant said that you are on holiday and that I should write a letter.

More details

The worst thing is that Mum and I cannot tighten the saddle, no matter how hard we try. This means that it moves slightly as I am riding along. I think you would agree that this is very dangerous.

There are other problems as well. The bell is stiff and doesn't ring properly, the brakes on the back wheel are rubbing and the left-hand pedal squeaks.

Conclusion

As I had to save for a long time to buy my bike at a rather high price, I'm sure you will agree that these things should be put right.

Letter ending

Yours sincerely,

Name of writer

Jennie Lindman

Think about it

In her letter, Jennie is trying to persuade Mr Smith to fix her bike. Imagine that one of the presents you have been given recently is not working as it should. Write a letter of complaint, like Jennie's, to the shop or to the manufacturer explaining the problem and persuading them to do something to put things right.

Remember to work in this way:
1. First jot down some brief notes of what you want to say.
2. Then draft your letter in handwriting or on your computer.
3. Next, edit the letter, looking carefully at your spelling and punctuation.
4. Finally, write your letter in your best handwriting or revise it on your computer.

Now try these

1. The headteacher of your school has asked you to write saying whether you are in favour or against having a school uniform.
   First decide if you are for or against school uniforms.
   Then write a letter giving your point of view and reasons for it.
2. You have heard that the Council is soon to close down your local library. Write a letter trying to persuade them to keep it open.

Looking at advertisements

This activity shows you how advertisers use language in a different way to catch attention.

Claims about the product

Name of product

Catchy language

Famous person says it's good

Think about it

Write a sentence to answer each of these questions.

1. What is being advertised?
2. Why do you think the word NEW is in capitals?
3. Can you really tell from this advert exactly how much goodness Weetibangs contain?
4. Can you tell whether Weetibangs are actually better for you than any other cereal?
5. Why do you think the advertisers use a picture and words of a famous swimming coach on the advert?
6. There are several catchy phrases in the advert. Which do you think is the best? Write another catchy phrase that might have been used in this advert, saying what a good taste the cereal has.

Now try these

Make up an advertisement to sell 'Speedsters', a new bike that is supposed to be the best designed ever.

1. First, make notes about the important things your advert should tell the readers.
2. Next, write some catchy phrases. You might even invent some of your own words.
3. Finally, design the advertisement using eye-catching colours and pictures.

Making a summary

This activity asks you to write a shorter version of this report.

> **Key words and phrases underlined**

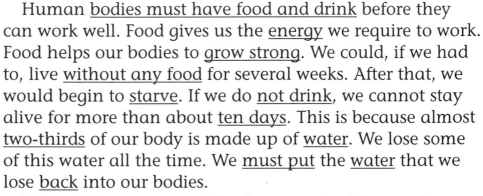

Human <u>bodies must have food and drink</u> before they can work well. Food gives us the <u>energy</u> we require to work. Food helps our bodies to <u>grow strong</u>. We could, if we had to, live <u>without any food</u> for several weeks. After that, we would begin to <u>starve</u>. If we do <u>not drink</u>, we cannot stay alive for more than about <u>ten days</u>. This is because almost <u>two-thirds</u> of our body is made up of <u>water</u>. We lose some of this water all the time. We <u>must put</u> the <u>water</u> that we lose <u>back</u> into our bodies.

Many different types of food are required for good health because food contains body-building materials. Body-building materials, like proteins, are found in foods such as meat, fish, cheese and nuts. Children need proteins to help them grow. Adults need proteins to repair any damage to their skin or bones. Fruit, dairy foods, vegetables and oils contain vitamins. Vitamins are the materials that help the body to fight against diseases. Foods like bread and rice help to give us energy. Fatty foods, like butter and oils, help to keep us warm. We also need small amounts of several minerals. These are found in many foods.

People have not always known that they need to eat different types of food to stay healthy. They thought it was good enough to eat any food that filled them up. Many people had crooked bones, bad eyesight or bad teeth. They did not eat enough of the right kinds of food. They did not store food properly or handle it carefully. As a result, men and women often lived only twenty or thirty years. Many children died from diseases before they were five years old. There are still many places in the world where people cannot afford the kind of food they require to stay healthy. They cannot keep food fresh or get clean water. Therefore, many people get sick and many children die.

In the past, no one knew that germs live in dirty water and dirty food. These germs cause many diseases. Often, food was stored in dirty pots and touched by unwashed hands. Often, milk was watered down with dirty water.

Think about it

1. There are four paragraphs in the passage about food.
   Read each paragraph again, and then in no more than one sentence write what each is about. The first one has been done to help you.

   Paragraph 1: Introduction about our bodies needing food and water.
   Paragraph 2:
   Paragraph 3:
   Paragraph 4:

2. The key words and phrases in the first paragraph are underlined. Write the key words for each of the other paragraphs. The first one has been done to help you.

   bodies must have food and drink, energy – grow strong,

   without any food, starve, not drink ten days, two-thirds water, must put water back

3. There are about 100 words in the first paragraph. Write a summary of it in not more than 35 words. Make sure you include all the most important information.

4. In not more than six interesting sentences, write a summary of the whole article. Use the work that you did in 'Think about it' to help you.

Now try these

1. Write a summary of this article.
   Try to use about 100 words.

Vegetables are an important part of our diet. Many people eat nothing but vegetables and fruit. Sometimes vegetables are cooked on their own, or added to soups, stews and sauces. The part that is eaten may be a root, like a carrot. It may be a stem, like asparagus, or a bulb, like an onion. Leaves, such as cabbage and lettuce, are also vegetables. Seeds, such as peas, or flowers, such as cauliflower, are also eaten as vegetables. Some fruits that are not sweet are often said to be vegetables. These include avocados, peppers and tomatoes.

Early people in Europe and Asia found peas, beans, onions, garlic, leeks and cabbage growing wild. All these were eaten in Roman times. The Romans also grew many other vegetables, such as pumpkins and turnips.

Until about 400 years ago, most people had to eat only the vegetables that grew near where they lived. Then the traders brought new foods back from their travels. At first they brought only root crops because these kept longer. The first carrots were brought to Europe from Afghanistan. They were purple. Carrots were so unusual that women used the feathery green tops to trim their hats. Today we can buy all sorts of vegetables and fruit from all over the world in our local shops.

2. Here are some key words and phrases. Write a paragraph that includes them.

   hungry; sign; need food; to live; also enjoyable;
   sharing food equals friendship